DATE DUE			
~~JAN 7 1975~~			
~~✗~~			
~~SS~~			
~~NO 18 99~~			
~~JR~~			
~~BB~~			
~~RM~~			
GAYLORD M-2			PRINTED IN U.S.A.

The Virginia Colony

THE VIRGINIA COLONY

by Harry Edward Neal

Illustrated by Jules Gotlieb

Hawthorn Books, Inc.
Publishers   New York

WL 296   9/71
THE VIRGINIA COLONY

First Edition: 1969

With love to my new,
beautiful, and first
granddaughter,
Karen Ellen Dinsenbacher

Contents

I

A Mystery of History

One of the world's most mysterious disappearances took place in Virginia.

A group of 117 men, women, and children vanished completely from a settlement on Roanoke Island. No one ever discovered when, where, why, or how they went. To this day, the mystery of the "Lost Colony" has not been solved.

The story begins in England in 1584 when Sir Walter Raleigh, an English explorer, wanted to start settlements in the New World. Raleigh obtained a charter from Queen

1

Elizabeth to begin a colony in any unsettled part of North America. Then he sent out two ships to explore the new country. Among those aboard was young Thomas Hariot, who was appointed by Raleigh to be surveyor and historian.

They landed near what is now Cape Hatteras in North Carolina.

Hariot later described their arrival:

Because of the many islands on the seacoast, it was difficult to discover an entry to the mainland. We found a large number of river mouths, yet they proved to be so shallow and full of dangerous sandbanks that we could not follow them up into the interior. Before we came upon an entrance, we made many attempts at different places and had sailed only a short way when we reached a broad river that descended in waterfalls into the sound opposite the islands. The shallows prevented us from going far up this stream; for the mouth of the river was choked with the sands that the tide drove in. Sailing farther, we reached a large island.

As soon as the inhabitants of this island caught sight of us, they set up a loud and terrible outcrying, as if they had never before seen men dressed as we were, and they ran off screaming like beasts and yelling like madmen. But we called them gently back and offered them presents, such as glass, knives, dolls and other trifles which we thought would please them. Convinced of our good intentions and kindness, they slowly approached and made us welcome. They took us to their island village, called "Roanoke," and to their Weroans, or chiefs, who entertained us courteously in spite of their astonishment at our appearance.

Hariot and the other Englishmen stayed on Roanoke Island for only a short time. When they sailed for England, two friendly Indians, named Manteo and Wanchese, agreed to go with them.

The ships' captains told Sir Walter Raleigh and the queen that they had seen a wonderful new and rich land.

"The place is a paradise!" they said.

"Is it big?" Raleigh asked.

"Yes, yes—very big. It is bounded on the east side by the ocean, on the south by Florida, and on the north by Nova Francea. As for the west, the limits are unknown."

They brought Manteo and Wanchese before the queen. "These are two of the people who inhabit the land. They are primitive, but friendly." Later the two Indians became a curiosity and a favorite topic among the English in London. One account says that Manteo returned to Roanoke and in 1587 was baptised as a Christian. It is probable that Wanchese also went back to the colony. Today there are towns of Manteo and Wanchese in North Carolina, named for these friendly Indians.

Although the two ships had sailed only to the coasts of what is now North Carolina, Queen Elizabeth decided that the new land should be called Virginia. She chose this name in her own honor, for she was unmarried and known to her subjects as the Virgin Queen.

In 1585 Raleigh sent 108 men to settle permanently in the new land. They dropped anchor off Roanoke Island at the mouth of Albemarle Sound. Although they stayed there for a few months, they were unhappy. Instead of building homes and planting crops, they went exploring, hoping to find gold and precious stones. They found none, and they used up most of the food they had brought with them. When the Indians refused to give or sell them corn, the white men burned the Indians' cornfields. The Indians then became their enemies, killed some of the settlers, and tried to drive the others away.

By 1586 the settlers had little food left. Many were sick and too weak to work. One day some English ships anchored near the island. They were commanded by Sir Francis Drake, a British officer and explorer, who had been fighting against the Spanish. He was on his way back to England and agreed to take the settlers along.

They carried with them some potatoes and Indian corn, which were unknown in England. They also took some tobacco that had been grown by the Indians. (Sir Walter Raleigh planted the potatoes on his estate in Ireland. Later they became the chief food of the Irish, and even today we call them "Irish potatoes.")

Raleigh still wanted to start a colony in Virginia, so in 1587 he sent 150 men, women, and children across the sea in three ships. They were led by Governor John White. This time they were supposed to go to the Chesapeake Bay, but the ships' captains put the passengers ashore on Roanoke Island and sailed away with two of the vessels. The third was left at the island.

The people began to build crude log cabins, but they soon realized that they would need many more supplies than they had brought with them. It was decided that Governor White should go back to England to get more help and more provisions.

About a week before he sailed, the governor became a grandfather. His daughter, Eleanor, was the wife of Ananias Dare, one of the governor's assistants. On August 18, 1587, she gave birth to a baby girl whom she named Virginia, in honor of the new land. Virginia Dare was the first child born of English parents in America.

Because the island was swampy, the men of the colony

wanted to move fifty miles into the mainland. When Governor White was about to leave for England, this proposed move was being considered.

"If you do move away," the governor said, "carve on a tree the name of your destination. Then when I come back I'll know where you've gone." After a moment's thought he added, "If you have trouble or distress, carve a cross above the name."

Some of the settlers returned to England with the governor. When they sailed, they left eighty-nine men, seventeen women, and eleven boys and girls on the island.

When Governor White reached home, he discovered that England was at war with Spain. The Spanish Armada, a huge fleet of warships, was preparing to sail against the British, and every ship in England was being made ready to fight.

Sir Walter Raleigh and Governor White tried in vain to send ships to the little colony across the seas. The Spanish fleet was eventually defeated by the English, but three years passed before the governor was able to return to Roanoke Island. In August 1590 he sailed as a passenger on one of three ships that took him to the colony by way of the West Indies.

At Roanoke Island, White went ashore with Captain Cooke and some of the ship's crew.

"As we went inshore up the sandy bank," the governor later reported, "we saw a tree on the brow of the cliff curiously carved with the clear Roman letters C R O. We knew at once that these letters indicated the place to which the planters had gone."

At the settlement, White discovered that all cabins had been destroyed. The ground was overgrown with high grass and weeds. The colony had been abandoned for at least a year.

5

At the right side of the entrance to the settlement, the bark had been stripped from a tree. Five feet above the ground, in clear capital letters, the word CROATOAN was carved in the wood. There was no cross or other sign of distress.

Croatoan, or Croatan, was the name of an island south of Roanoke Island where Croatoan Indians lived. Governor White believed that the people of the colony had gone there, because he knew that the Croatoans were friendly to the settlers.

The next morning Captain Cooke agreed to sail to Croatoan to search for the settlers. As the crew raised one of two anchors, the cable broke and the ship drifted until it was almost grounded. They managed to reach deeper water, but then a storm came up. The ship's food supply was very low, and there was only one cask of fresh water, so the captain decided to go to St. John or some other island where they could get provisions. After that, they intended to make the voyage to Croatoan.

The ship ran into bad weather and finally reached Flores Island in the Azores. There the captain decided not to go to Croatoan, but to return home instead. His ship docked at Plymouth, England, on October 24, 1590.

Sir Walter Raleigh sent expeditions to America to find the Roanoke Island colonists, but somehow none of the search parties ever visited the Croatoan Indian village. Many years later, Indians in that area were found to have some physical characteristics of the white man, such as blond hair. Some people think these were descendants of Roanoke Islanders who had intermarried with the Indians. This is only a guess, and what really became of the members of the Lost Colony is still a mystery of history.

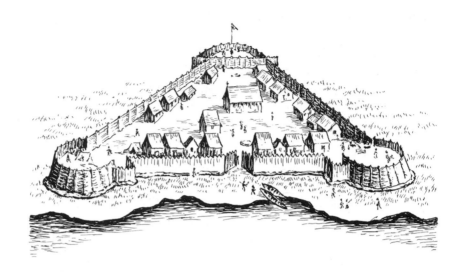

2

The Pitiful Pioneers

After the people of the Lost Colony vanished, the Indians on Roanoke Island saw no more white settlers for many years.

Queen Elizabeth died in 1603, and England was now ruled by King James I. In 1606 he permitted a group of wealthy men to form the London Company. These men believed that Virginia was rich in gold and jewels, so they made up a new expedition to go there and found a colony. Of course, the

London Company expected the settlers to send any treasure they found back to England.

On December 31, 1606, three sailing ships left England. They were named the *Susan Constant,* the *Godspeed,* and the *Discovery.* All three were under the command of Captain Christopher Newport.

In addition to the crews and supplies, the ships carried 104 men. There were no women passengers. Some of the men were experienced miners whose job would be to mine gold. Some were carpenters, who could build cabins. More than fifty were gentlemen who had never done any real work. They expected to find gold and precious stones and take them back to England. A number of soldiers went along to help protect the settlers from unfriendly Indians.

One of the passengers was a young man named John Smith. He was handsome, with bright blue eyes, wavy red hair, a bushy red beard, and a long pointed red mustache. Although he was only twenty-seven years old, John Smith already had a reputation as a swashbuckler, a soldier of fortune, and a fearless fighter. His adventures began when he left home at the age of sixteen, and he had been through so many hair-raising dangers and escapes that some people said he led a charmed life.

John Smith had persuaded many of the settlers to make the voyage to Virginia. He believed they had a good chance to make a new life with a better future than they could find in England.

The three ships ran into heavy storms that slowed them down. The passengers grew restless. They quarreled for little or no reason.

One day Smith told the men, "You should stop this nonsense. We ought to be planning what's to be done when we reach Virginia. Who's going to be our leader there? Who's to be on the council?"

One of the gentlemen said, "Oh, so that's it? You want to be in command."

Edward Maria Wingfield, a member of the London Company, disliked Smith. Wingfield said, "Not just in command. He wants to be king of Virginia!"

Smith glared at Wingfield and the others. "Fools!" he said, then turned and strode away.

Everyone knew that Captain Newport had a sealed envelope in which King James had placed the names of seven men to be members of the council to govern the new colony. Smith asked the captain to open the envelope so the council might be organized while they were still at sea.

"I will not, sir!" Captain Newport told him. "My orders are to open the envelope after we go ashore in Virginia, and that's what I shall do."

As the days passed, Smith tried to get his fellow passengers to join him in a demand that Captain Newport open the sealed envelope. Edward Wingfield spread the false rumor that Smith wanted to take over the ship and force the passengers to recognize him as king of Virginia. Many of the men believed Wingfield and told Captain Newport that Smith was dangerous. Newport had Smith arrested and put in irons until the voyage ended.

But the voyage did not end as soon as they had hoped. The ships were at sea for nearly four months. On April 26, 1607, a lookout cried, "Land, ho!" The passengers rushed to the rail and cheered. They had finally reached Virginia.

Captain Newport and some of the men went ashore, but only for a little while. They found that this was a point of land, a cape, and they named it Cape Henry in honor of the eldest son of King James. They made a wooden cross and stuck it into the ground. Then Captain Newport said, "We claim this land in the name of the Church of England and King James the First."

The newcomers were suddenly attacked by unfriendly Indians. The noise of the English guns frightened the savages, and the men managed to return to the ship before anyone was hurt.

They sailed up a river which they named the James River in honor of King James. On May 14, 1607, they came to the place where they decided to settle. The crews moored the three ships to trees along the riverbanks, and the men went ashore.

The corners of a square of canvas were tied to tree trunks to make a crude shelter. Under it the minister, Reverend Robert Hunt, offered a prayer of thanks for their safe arrival. They decided that the place should be called Jamestown, though it was also known later as James City.

When Captain Newport opened the sealed box containing the names of those who were to govern the colony, he learned that they consisted of the captain himself, Edward Maria Wingfield, Bartholomew Gosnold, John Ratcliffe, John Martin, George Kendall—and a surprise—Captain John Smith!

"Not Smith!" Wingfield said. "He can't be trusted. You all know he wants to set himself up as king."

So it was agreed that Smith would not be allowed to serve on the council. Wingfield was elected council president.

In exploring the new land, the settlers came to an Indian village where they received a friendly welcome. The Indians gave them corn, pumpkins, oysters, and tobacco and showed them which wild berries were good to eat.

The colonists lived in tents while some of them cut down

11

trees to build a fort and cabins. Many of the gentlemen, wearing their silk coats and trousers, with lace ruffles at their necks and wrists, went off to search for gold and jewels.

One day Captain John Smith, with twenty of the settlers, set out to explore the Chickahominy River. They traveled as far as the place where the city of Richmond now stands. There Smith wandered away from the others. He was seized by a band of Indians who took him to the camp of their chief, Powhatan, on the York River.

Powhatan was a powerful leader, the emperor of thirty Indian tribes. He was very old. A few long strands of white hair hung down from his headdress of eagle feathers, and he wore a robe made of raccoon skins.

About four hundred braves and squaws watched Smith as he was greeted by Powhatan. One Indian woman brought a bowl of water in which Smith washed his hands. Another woman gave him a bundle of feathers to use as a towel.

Powhatan ordered food to be brought, and Smith was given a feast of turkey and venison. Then the Indians sat in council and decided that Smith should be killed.

They brought in two big flat stones and made Smith lie down with his head on the rocks. A big Indian with a heavy club prepared to smash the white man's skull.

Suddenly, an Indian girl dashed out of the crowd and fell to her knees, her body across Smith's back. She was Powhatan's daughter. Her name was Matoaka, which means "a bright stream between two hills," but she was also called Pocahontas. According to John Smith's own account, she was "sixteen or eighteen years old." She wore a dress of deerskin, and in her black hair was a single white heron feather.

Pocahontas pleaded with her father to spare Smith's life. Powhatan agreed, and Smith was set free to return to Jamestown.

Some people say this incident never happened. John Smith wrote two books about his experiences in Jamestown, but in his first account he said nothing about being saved by Pocahontas. In his second book he told the story about her, but some historians think he made up most of it. The fact is, however, that there was a real Indian princess named Pocahontas who later played a part in the story of Jamestown.

When he returned to the settlement, Smith discovered that Edward Wingfield had been plotting against him. Wingfield wanted to send Smith back to England with Captain Newport, who was preparing to leave the colony.

"Why should I return to England?" Smith wanted to know.

"To avoid the disgrace of a trial," Wingfield said.

"A trial for what?"

"For conspiring to set yourself up as king of Virginia!"

Smith smiled and said, "On the contrary, sir, I demand a trial—and I want it here and now! Now!"

So Captain Smith was tried at Jamestown. From his testimony and statements of many of the colonists, the jury declared that he was not guilty. The jury also decided that Edward Wingfield must pay Smith two hundred pounds for false imprisonment. To make this payment, Wingfield had to give up all of his property to Smith, but Smith turned it over to the colony for the good of all.

Now the colonists began to see John Smith in a new light. He was a professional soldier, he was fearless, he had explored the river and met Powhatan. Smith was given his seat on the council and looked upon as a leader.

On June 22 Captain Newport sailed for England, leaving 104 men at Jamestown. He promised to return with more colonists and supplies.

The men built a small triangular fort and planted a field

of corn, but the summer days grew hot and damp, and the settlers were not used to this kind of climate. Their food supplies were low. Some tried to steal from the Indians, and the Indians grew angry. There were skirmishes in which the Indians were frightened off by the English guns.

The water was not fit to drink. At high tide the river was salty. At low tide the water was slimy and dirty.

Mosquitoes came out of the nearby swamps, carrying malaria germs into the colony. There was little medicine, and Dr. Thomas Wotton was helpless in treating the sick. Scores of men shivered with chills and burned with fevers. Even those who had no disease became sick for lack of food. Many died.

In his diary one colonist wrote, "God plagued us with such famine and sickness that the living were scarce able to bury the dead. Our men were destroyed with cruell diseases, but for the most part they died of meere famine. Our food was but a small Can of Barlie sod in water to five men a day."

Sick and dying men groaned in every corner of the fort, night and day. Death came to three or four every night, and their bodies "were trailed out of their Cabines like Dogges, to be buried. . . . From May to September, those that escaped lived upon sea crabs and sturgeon. Fifty in this time we buried."

The sick and the dead put the settlers at the mercy of the Indians, and they expected Indian attacks that never came. Instead, the Indians took pity and brought them meat and corn and fruits.

John Smith tried to cheer everyone, and they looked to him to save what was left of the settlement. He ordered some men to build houses, some to bind rushes to make thatched roofs, others to clear away brush and trees.

He took beads, mirrors, and hatchets to Chief Powhatan

and traded them for meat and corn, which saved some of the colonists from starvation.

On a freezing cold January 14, 1608, a cry went up from the fort: "Ships! Ships are coming!"

Captain Newport had come back, as he had promised, bringing 120 men and some supplies, including a few live pigs and chickens. The newcomers were greeted with laughter and hearty handshakes as they were bombarded with questions about happenings in England. The colonists were cheerful as they unloaded the food, clothing, and ammunition which the ships had brought.

Their happiness didn't last long. On January 17, only three days after the ships had arrived, fire broke out in one of the buildings where the supplies were stored. The wind spread the flames to other buildings. Soon most of the little settlement was destroyed.

Captain Smith tried to make the men rebuild the houses. Some of the gentlemen found some shiny yellow particles. Gold! Gold fever swept the settlement. As one colonist wrote, "There is no talke, no hope, no worke, but dig gold, wash gold, refine gold." Unfortunately, the gold was only worthless iron pyrites—fool's gold.

Captain Newport, preparing to sail for England again, wanted to load his ships with dirt that might contain gold. Smith objected, saying that the amount of gold in a shipload of dirt would be very small, and there might be no gold at all. Instead of the dirt, Smith had the ships loaded with cedar logs and other timber, which could be sold at a profit in England. Captain Newport grumbled but sailed away with his cargo of wood.

During that winter, scores of the settlers died. Some were frozen to death, others were victims of disease.

In June, John Smith and fourteen other men sailed up river

on a voyage of discovery and to find food. John Ratcliffe was appointed president of the council.

Smith and his companions explored the Potomac River and Chesapeake Bay. They traded with some Indians for food and had to fight others who were hostile. When they returned to Jamestown on July 21, they found most of the men sick; many, dying. The settlers were angry about Ratcliffe.

"He took more than his share of our food," some said. "He's hiding provisions in his house."

"Not only that," others said. "He's had men building him a big house—a regular palace."

Smith seized Ratcliffe's provisions and divided them among the colonists. He also ordered the men to stop working on Ratcliffe's palace.

Once again, Smith and twelve men went on an expedition into unknown country. When they returned on September 7, they found more settlers dead and others dying from yellow fever. Those who were not sick were put to work repairing buildings in which they could store the supplies they expected from England.

Captain Newport brought few provisions on his second supply trip, but he did bring seventy new colonists. They included the first two English women to come to Jamestown— Mrs. Thomas Forrest and her maid, Ann Burras.

John Smith gave Captain Newport a letter to take back to England in December 1608. In it, Smith said that the London Company must send more food and fewer gentlemen. They must, he wrote, "send thirty carpenters, husbandmen, gardeners, fishermen, blacksmiths, masons, and diggers-up of tree roots," along with food enough to keep them alive.

The year 1608 was a happy one for at least two of the colonists. John Laydon, a carpenter who had come to Jamestown in 1607, married Ann Burras—the first wedding in Virginia. A year later their first child was born. They named her Virginia, and she was the first white baby born in Jamestown.

Food was getting scarce again. About half of the supply of corn rotted in storage, and much of the other half was eaten by rats that had crossed the sea on the English ships. The people were sick and desperate.

John Smith called the colonists together. "From now on," he said, "every man who is not disabled by illness will be expected to do his full share of work. He who does not work will not eat! Our food supply is low, so we must gather for ourselves the fruits the earth doth yield." He shook a warning finger at them and added, "And he that gathereth not every day as much as I do, the next day shall be set beyond the river and banished from this fort as a drone, till he amend his conditions or starve."

Even the gentlemen began to blister their hands using hoes and axes. Soon the men had rebuilt a number of houses, dug a well that provided good water, erected a church and a blockhouse, and planted about thirty acres of land in corn and wheat.

But disease continued to strike down the colonists, and there were several incidents that made the Indians more and more unfriendly. Some settlers attacked Indian women. Others stole Indian food. Hatred was growing on both sides.

In England there was an economic depression and thousands had no work. Many decided to go to America to make a new life. Some, however, were criminals who were forced to go against their will. The king thought this was a good way to rid the country of undesirables. A few of these outlaws committed suicide rather than be sent to Jamestown.

Although Jamestown was the center of activity, the colony of Virginia covered a vast territory. Under a royal charter of 1609, it spread over what are now the states of Virginia,

Kentucky, Ohio, Indiana, Illinois, Wisconsin, West Virginia, and part of Minnesota. There was land enough for everybody.

On June 18, 1609, nine ships sailed from England, bound for Jamestown. They started out with five hundred men, women, and children. Scores died at sea of fever and plague. One ship sank in a storm with all on board. One was blown ashore in Bermuda. Quantities of provisions the ships carried were ruined by salt water. The remaining seven ships reached Jamestown in August, with only three hundred people.

One day, while John Smith and other men were in a small boat, a can of gunpowder exploded, and Smith was badly burned. In October he decided to go to England to have his burns treated. When Smith said goodbye to the colonists, Jamestown consisted of about fifty houses, a main fort, and five smaller forts. There were nearly five hundred people, a few hundred hogs, sheep, goats, and chickens, and six horses.

Smith never returned to Virginia, though he made other voyages. He died in England in 1631.

John Smith thought the Jamestown settlers could continue without too many hardships. He was wrong. After he had sailed away, disaster struck. The Indians, who had feared and respected Smith, attacked the forts and murdered many settlers. They stole guns, food, and clothing.

This was what has been called "the starving time" in Jamestown. Each person was given only five kernels of corn a day, until all of the corn had been eaten. The people killed and ate all the livestock, including the horses. Within six short months there were only sixty people left of the five hundred who were there when John Smith sailed for England. The other four hundred and forty had been killed by disease, by the Indians, or by starvation. According to one account, the sixty survivors were "most miserable and poore creatures, and those were preserved for the most part by roots, herbes, acornes, walnuts, berries, and now and then a little fish."

In June 1610, at the peak of this period of suffering, the settlers who had been shipwrecked in Bermuda arrived in two vessels, the *Patience* and the *Deliverance*. The ships' commanders, Sir Thomas Gates and Sir George Somers, were so horrified when they saw the weak, sick, and starving colonists that they decided to take everybody back to England.

So Jamestown was completely abandoned on June 7, 1610. The colonists and the newcomers were aboard the ships on the James River, bound for the open sea and England. But, before they reached the ocean, they met three other English ships heading for Jamestown. They were carrying the newly appointed governor, Lord De La Warr, more settlers, and great quantities of food and other supplies.

Lord De La Warr persuaded the departing colonists to return. On June 10, 1610, they all sailed back to Jamestown —and this time they were there to stay.

3

Law, Love, and Labor

One day in 1613 some young boys and girls were playing blindman's buff near the church in Jamestown. One boy suddenly pointed towards the woods.

"Look!" he cried. "It's Cap'n Argall—and Pocahontas!"

Captain Samuel Argall was an English soldier and explorer who would later be governor of Jamestown. With his men he had asked Chief Powhatan to trade for food, but Powhatan had refused. After leaving the Indian camp, Argall met Pocahontas on the trail and took her prisoner.

Pocahontas was well-known to the colonists, for she had come to the settlement often after John Smith's visit to her father's camp.

A number of men and women surrounded Argall and the girl, asking why she was a captive.

"Her father refused to trade with us," Argall said. "We'll hold the girl as hostage until he changes his mind."

But Powhatan didn't change his mind, and Pocahontas stayed with the colonists for many weeks. During that time, she was taught about the Christian faith by the Reverend Alexander Whitaker. When the people agreed that she should be allowed to return to her native village, she refused.

"I wish to live here," she said. "I wish to be a Christian."

So Pocahontas was baptised by Mr. Whitaker and adopted by the colony. She was christened Rebecca, and because she was a princess, the daughter of an Indian emperor, she was entitled to be called Lady Rebecca.

One colonist in particular took an interest in her. He was John Rolfe, a settler who was studying the cultivation of tobacco. He and Pocahontas fell in love, and in April 1614 they were married in the Jamestown church.

The wedding was a festive occasion. The gentlemen, or cavaliers, wore doublets (a kind of blouse) of green, blue, or red silk or satin, with loose-flowing sleeves. Around their necks were falling bands of Vandyke lace. Loose trousers were fastened below the knee with fancy garters. Their hats had wide brims, gold or silver hatbands, and some were decorated with white plumes.

Because of danger from Indian attacks, many of the men wore light armor, such as chain mail or breastplates, and carried swords and guns. Most of the cavaliers had long hair, pointed beards, and neat mustaches. A few wore beads and single earrings. Their shoes were of leather, with large gold or silver buckles.

The ordinary settler's costume was drab by contrast. His daily dress was of coarse brown wool, called frieze, but for the wedding he wore his Sunday best. This was good broadcloth, brightened by gilded or silver buttons. Instead of armor, he wore a leather jerkin, or jacket, thick enough to slow down an Indian arrow or a knife. A few also wore leather breeches. His doublet was of homespun, or canvas, or perhaps of linen.

Many of the women were more colorfully dressed than the gentlemen. Some wore gowns of silk or satin or velvet, colored bright green, sky blue, scarlet, gold, or olive. Around their necks were wide and high white pleated collars, heavily starched, called ruffs. Some of the ladies looked as though they were being choked by the ruffs.

Some ladies wore large, soft slouch hats with the brims turned up or down. Some simply covered their heads with the hoods of cloaks. Many wore necklaces and rings of diamonds, emeralds, or other jewels. Their shoes were of silk, velvet, or soft leather, decorated with colorful rosettes. Their fancy clothes, of course, had been brought from England.

The children were dressed in costumes like those of their fathers and mothers—and most of the boys and girls seemed quite uncomfortable as they sat quietly in the church. Powhatan did not go to the wedding, but he sent Pocahontas's two brothers and her uncle. The wedding helped to improve relations with Powhatan and his tribes, although many Indians still refused to be friendly.

John Rolfe continued the experiments he had started in 1611 in growing tobacco. The tobacco used by the Indians was a wild weed and too strong to make an enjoyable smoke. The best tobacco was grown in Trinidad and Venezuela, and Rolfe imported some of each kind, which he planted in Jamestown. Then he crossbred one with another until he finally developed what became known as the Virginia leaf. This was mild and had a distinctive taste and smell. When Rolfe first shipped some of it to England in 1613, it was highly praised. The English asked for more.

The Rolfes lived in Rolfe's home, Varina, on the James River. There, Pocahontas bore their only child, a son, Thomas Rolfe.

In 1616 Pocahontas, John, and Thomas Rolfe sailed to England. There Lady Rebecca Rolfe was received and entertained as the Indian princess she was. In England the Rolfes were a happy family—but not for long. The damp and chilly English climate made Mrs. Rolfe ill, and she died in England in 1617. John Rolfe went back to Jamestown, and later his son Thomas joined him there. John Rolfe resumed his work with tobacco.

At first the Virginia tobacco crop was small. As the demand grew, more land was devoted to growing tobacco, and in 1617 about twenty thousand pounds were shipped to England. This was still not enough to meet the demand for it, and by 1619 the shipments had increased to more than forty thousand pounds. Now the colonists were sure that tobacco was a commercial success, and a great new industry had begun.

Tobacco was fast becoming the money of the colony. So great was the demand that almost every settler tried to grow tobacco. Some plants even grew in the streets of Jamestown!

Strangely enough, King James hated tobacco. "It is lothesome to the eye," he said, "hateful to the Nose, harmefull to the brain, dangerous to the lungs, and in the blacke stinking fume thereof, nearest resembling the horrible Stigian smoke of the pit that is bottomless." All the same, it was very valuable.

As Jamestown grew from a village into a town, the colonists began to build forts and houses in outlying areas. One of these places was called Kecougtan, later renamed Elizabeth City. One was at Cape Henry. Near the falls on the James River the town of Henricus (Henrico) was founded, followed by Charles City. All four places were called cities, and all were controlled by the London Company.

While these cities were being established, the London Company also granted permission to groups of its stockholders to start new settlements along the James River and east and west from it. Parcels of one hundred acres of land were given to these groups, and their settlements were called particular plantations. Sometimes they were also called hundreds, because of the hundred-acre allotments of land, or because the groups usually consisted of one hundred settlers. Seven of these plantations were established by 1619.

The colony was growing, and Jamestown was its center. The year 1619 saw three important happenings in the colony —one dealing with law and order, one with love, and the other with labor.

The law and order was made possible by the action of a court in England. On November 28, 1618, the court had approved "The Great Charter of Privileges, Orders, and Laws." It was largely the work of Sir Edwin Sandys, who has been called the father of representative government in America.

In 1619 Sir George Yardley was sent to Jamestown as governor to get the new system started. On July 30, 1619, the First General Assembly of Virginia met in Jamestown. It consisted of the governor, the council, and a House of Burgesses. A burgess was simply a citizen chosen by the people

in an election district to represent them in the assembly. (Today these representatives are called delegates.) In 1619 there were two burgesses from each of eleven election districts, making a total of twenty-two members of the House of Burgesses.

Laws made by the House of Burgesses were sent to England for approval by the king but were in effect until the king's decision was received.

That first assembly was in session only from July 30 to August 4, 1619. It adjourned "by reason of extreme heat." This was an important meeting, because it was the very first example of representative government in America and the Western World. It led the way to our present state legislatures and to the Congress of the United States.

Most of the colonists were men. Some women were there, but they were married and had children. Many single men quarreled with each other and wanted to go back to England. The London Company decided that if these men had wives, they would stop fighting and would build homes and raise families. Then they would stay in the colony and help to make it grow and prosper. So in 1619 the company got together a number of unmarried girls who were willing to go to Virginia to become wives.

From 1619 to 1621 about 150 girls left England for the Virginia Colony. In Virginia they were expected, but not forced, to marry. They lived with families until such time as the girls found husbands. Most of them married tobacco planters. When a planter took a bride, he gave the company 120 pounds of tobacco as payment for her passage from England. Later this price was raised to 150 pounds. By 1622 practically all of the maidens had been wed.

Other people who came from England were indentured servants, called redemptioners. They paid for their passage by agreeing to work as servants for five or seven years. At the end of that time they were given land of their own on which they made homes, planted crops, and raised families.

One day in 1619 the colonists gathered at the waterfront to watch a strange ship that anchored at Jamestown. At first they thought it was a Dutch battleship, but when its captain and crew came ashore, the colonists discovered that they were pirates. They had come from Africa, where they had traded rum for twenty Negroes. They intended to sell the Negroes in the West Indies but said the ship had been blown off its course. Now they sold all twenty to the people of Jamestown and were paid in tobacco.

Although they were sold like merchandise, the Negroes were not yet treated as slaves. Some were put to work in the fields, and some became servants in the homes of the planters. They were expected to work to pay back money for their passage, just as white indentured servants did. Once the debt was paid, they were free men. Not until 1662 was the Negro treated as a slave.

More and more people were coming to Jamestown from England, but the company in London failed to send enough food and other supplies to take care of them properly. Many colonists chose to grow tobacco rather than food crops. Men, women, and children went hungry. Yellow fever and other diseases killed scores of victims. Then a greater disaster threatened to wipe out the colony completely, beginning with the plantations.

The Jamestown plantations extended for many miles away from the town itself. The planters had built brick houses and had made claim to hundreds of acres of land, where they grew tobacco. Powhatan, the Indian chief, had died. His successor was Opechancanough, who was afraid that the planters would take over all of the lands occupied by the Indians. On March 22, 1622, he decided to do something about it.

It was eight o'clock in the morning. There was a touch of spring in the air and no warning of danger. The people on the plantations were doing their usual chores. Suddenly the stillness was ripped by wild shrieks and whoops as hordes of Indians came crashing out of the woods, up and down the river. They rushed into houses and through the grounds. With tomahawks and knives and bows and arrows they killed men, women, and children. One victim of the attack was John Rolfe. A few Indians were killed too.

One young Indian who had become a Christian warned the people in the town itself against an attack on the fort. Guards were posted near all approaches. A number of Indians tried to fight their way in, but the guns of the settlers scared them away.

When the massacre began there were about a thousand people in the colony. When it ended, 347 of the colonists were dead—more than one-third of the entire population. Many others were wounded, and some of these died later.

When news of the tragedy reached King James in England, he used it as an excuse to put the London Company out of business. The real reason was that he thought the colonists were acting too independently. The company had not paid the profits it had hoped for, so the king decided to take over the Virginia Colony for himself.

On May 24, 1624, King James canceled the charter of the London Company, and Virginia became a Crown Colony —the first royal colony in the history of England. Its first royal governor was Sir Francis Wyatt, who was the company governor at the time the charter was revoked.

Jamestown itself was becoming the center of social and political life for the colony. The population had grown to about five thousand by 1625. At that time, according to *Jamestown, Virginia,* by Charles E. Hatch, Jr.:

Jamestown had a church, a court-of-guard [guard-house], three stores, a merchant's store, and thirty-three houses. Ten of its forty boats were here, including a skiff, a "shallop" of four tons, and a "barque" of forty tons. There were stores of fish (24,880 pounds), corn, peas, and meal. There were four cannon, supplies of powder, shot and lead, and, for individual use, "fixt pieces," snaphances [rifles], pistols, seventy swords, coats of mail, quilted coats, and suits of armor (thirty-five of them complete). The bulk of the colony's livestock seems to have been localized in the Jamestown area—about half (one hundred eighty-three) of the cattle, a little more than half (two hundred sixty-five) of the hogs, and well over half (one hundred twenty-six) of the goats. The one horse listed for the colony was at Jamestown.

Despite all of its troubles, the Virgina Colony was now a permanent settlement in the New World. It was to play a big and important part in the development of America.

4
Living and Learning

After the terrible massacre of 1622, the Indians made no more serious trouble for years. Jamestown families were growing, but there was no great rush of newcomers. Wild stories and rumors about the Indians scared many people who had considered leaving England for America.

A new law was made in 1637 to give fifty acres of land to any person who would build a house on it within two years. This helped to attract more people from across the

31

sea. A number of new homes were started. A few were in the town itself, but most were located along the river. They were small, perhaps having only one or two rooms. Some had clapboard sidings, but others were made of brick, and the bricks were made in the colony. Thatched roofs were common.

Most homes had simple furnishings, usually made by the colonists. Chairs were a novelty, even in some houses in England, so very few settlers owned a chair. People sat on stools and benches. Some of the benches were simply logs cut lengthwise, with the flat side up, and four straight legs under the curved bottom side.

Tables were generally made of long, thick oak boards. Some were supported by x-shaped trestles, called sawbucks, at each end; some, by two legs that looked like upside down T's connected by one long board.

Beds were rough frameworks holding mattresses filled with straw. Sometimes there were not enough beds to go around, so some members of the family slept on piles of straw on the floor. Wealthier families might have soft mattresses filled with feathers. A few had trundle beds for children, which were small enough to be kept under the larger beds during the daytime. A baby slept in a cradle near the fireplace.

Most early Virginia homes were so small that there was no room for closets. Some families made small cabinets in which they kept things such as medicines, wine, ink, and tobacco. Clothes were hung on wooden pegs stuck into the walls. Quilts, blankets, and linens were stored in chests that had hinged lids and that could also be used as seats if necessary.

The Jamestown colonists had no lamps for some time. At

night they burned tallow candles, although some people read, sewed or did other small chores with only the flickering light from the fireplace. They went to bed soon after dark and got up about dawn.

Some of the cavaliers had huge plantations for growing tobacco. They were given some of their land under the "head right" system. This provided that a colonist could receive fifty acres of ground for each person he brought to Virginia. Planters paid to bring servants from England. Also, planters who were shareholders in the London Company had been given one hundred acres of land for each share they owned. Some eventually owned a hundred thousand acres or more.

They first built their homes near the James River, then spread northward to the York, the Rappahannock and the Potomac. All four of these rivers flowed into Chesapeake Bay and boats could be used for transportation. Settlers who lived inland traveled on horseback, in homemade wagons, or in carriages shipped from England.

The House of Burgesses wanted to make new towns along the rivers. The planters objected. The planters controlled the land, and each plantation was its own little kingdom. It had its own boat docks and storage buildings, and its own vegetable gardens and livestock. Indentured servants worked in the fields and homes. Growing numbers of Negroes were brought to Jamestown and sold to the planters. Although many field hands on the big plantations were Negroes, they were still treated the same as the white servants.

The class system that existed in England was evident in the Virginia Colony. The gentlemen, or cavaliers, were considered the better sort and were entitled to be called Mister. The ordinary folk, or commoners, were the meaner sort.

33

They were called by their last names or by their occupations, such as carpenter, landlord, miller, tanner, cobbler, and so on.

Wives of the gentlemen were called Madam. Commoners' wives were called Goody.

Some of the commoners were tradesmen who raised tobacco, bought more land, or perhaps obtained more by bringing friends or relatives from England. As these tradesmen grew wealthier and enlarged their properties, they also came to be looked upon as gentlemen.

Tobacco was profitable, and for a while the colonists used their ground for almost nothing else. Food shortages made some of them realize that they must plant fruits and vegetables, so a few food crops increased.

For meat, they supplied Indians with guns and sent them to hunt deer and other game. The Indian hunters were paid in trinkets.

Many buildings were neglected. Even the church was ready to fall down, because everybody was busy planting tobacco. But tobacco took so much nourishment from the earth that after five or six years the soil was too poor for raising other crops. For this reason, people would abandon these sections and move to new locations to plant more tobacco. Lands that had been cleared by the Indians were taken over by the settlers to be used for tobacco fields.

Tobacco was loaded aboard ships that came to the docks of the big plantations. Small planters who lived inland packed their tobacco in huge barrels. The filled barrels were placed on their sides so they could be rolled. By means of a pole-axle and wooden frame, each barrel could be pulled by a horse or an ox to the loading dock to be put aboard a ship for transportation to England.

Some people believed that tobacco could prevent disease.

They pinned tobacco leaves to their clothing. Bunches of the leaves were hung on beds and chairs. In some homes, tobacco was burned in a bowl at mealtimes. Many people considered taking snuff and chewing tobacco health measures.

Since tobacco was like money in the colony, the council tried to limit the number of plants one family could grow. Also, tobacco that was of poor quality was burned so that it could not be put in and sold with good tobacco. Bad tobacco was like counterfeit money.

As land became exhausted by tobacco, planters moved to new locations and the area of the colony grew accordingly. Larger settlements began to form on the banks of the York and Rappahannock rivers. Soon it became necessary to lay out boundaries of shires, or counties. In 1634 there were eight of these—Accomack, Charles City, Charles River, or York, Elizabeth City, Henrico, James City, Warrasquoke, and Warwick.

The Indians were pushed farther and farther off their lands. In April 1644 the tribes banded together and swooped down upon the white men. Several hundred colonists were killed before the Indians were driven away.

The massacre did not keep the settlers from seeking new lands. By 1650 the Virginia frontier to the north and east had reached the Potomac River. But Jamestown was still considered the capital of the colony, which now numbered about seventeen thousand people. About three hundred of these were Negroes.

Newcomers from England were often surprised to discover that some features of the colony consisted of more than tobacco and Indians. When Mr. and Mrs. Jeffrey Williams and their son George reached Jamestown, George wandered around the town while his parents sought information about land. George was fourteen years old and was excited to be exploring his new world.

As he stopped at an open shed to watch a cooper and his helpers making barrel staves, another boy about his own age came up to him.

"Hello," the other boy said.

"Hello."

"I saw you at the dock. Didn't you just come from England?"

"Yes, with my mother and father," George said.

"You came on the same ship with Sir William Berkeley. He's our new governor."

"I know."

"What's your name?"

"George Williams. What's yours?"

"Frank—Frank Thomas. You going to live in Jamestown?"

"I don't know. It depends on my parents." George gazed up and down the street. "Are there really Indians around here? Are they as bad as people say?"

Frank smiled. "They're around, well enough. But they don't bother us in the town. Sometimes they make trouble for the tobacco planters up the river, though."

"My father says everybody in the colony must be a tobacco planter," George said.

"It was that way once," Frank answered. "But now people do other things. Come on, I'll show you."

They walked along the rough dirt street. Frank pointed to a wooden building and said, "Over there they make silk."

"Silk? I didn't know silk came from here. I thought it all came from Spain and France."

"I guess most of it still does. And from Italy too. They

37

raise silkworms on the mulberry trees here, but not many. My father says the silk they make here costs so much that nobody wants to buy it. He thinks they'll stop making it pretty soon."

George turned around and pointed up the street. "I saw those men working in the cooper's shop. It looks as though they're making a lot of barrels."

"They can't make 'em fast enough," Frank said. "They use an awful lot of them for shipping tobacco and wine."

"Wine? They make wine here too?"

"Oh, yes. And beer, too." Frank pointed to a distant field. "See out there? That's a big vineyard. Those are all grape-vines you see. There's a small tobacco patch there too, but it's mostly grapes for wine."

On the outskirts of the town a column of gray smoke curled skyward. George pointed to it and said, "There's a fire over there. It looks as though someone's house is burn-ing."

Frank laughed. "It's nobody's house. That's where they're making soap-ashes and potash. They have to burn a lot of trees and—"

"I know, I know. They burn the wood to ashes, and they use the ashes to make soap and glass. We learned about that in school back home." He paused, then asked, "They ship the potash to England—but do they make soap and glass here too?"

"Soap, but not much glass. They used to make glass, but it wasn't very good. They make more money by selling the ashes."

As the boys neared the river, they could see a few small boats near the shore, and men at work on the land.

"What are they doing?" George asked.

"Mending their nets. They get a lot of fish out of the river, but the nets get torn and have to be fixed."

"Don't they fish with hooks?"

"Oh, yes. Even I go fishing with hooks. But the men using the nets get a lot more fish to sell. They make their living that way."

A short, fat man with wild-looking brown hair and a round, red face came toward them. He carried several small cloth bags in each hand. He grinned at the boys and said, "Good morrow, Master Thomas." He nodded at George.

"Hello, Duncan," Frank said. "I see you've been collecting again."

Duncan kept walking as he answered, "A good thing it is too. If I stopped, we'd all be in trouble."

The boys watched him trudge toward the town. "What did he mean?" George asked. 'What's he collecting?"

"He collects herbs and plants for the doctors to use in making medicine. He keeps them separate in those little bags."

"What kinds of plants?" George asked.

"Oh, bloodwort, wintergreen, sassafras, bayberries, rhubarb—a lot of things like that."

For a little while the boys watched the fishermen mending their nets. Then George said, "Say! I've got to get back in town. My parents will be looking for me."

They started back. On the way, George saw a small, round brick building that he hadn't noticed before. It had a cone-shaped wooden roof, one door, and no windows. "That's a funny looking building," he said. "It doesn't have any windows."

Frank laughed. "If it did, it wouldn't be much good. That's an icehouse. In the winter we cut cakes of ice out of the river and store them in there to use in the hot weather. If there was a window, the sun would melt the ice."

"What do you do with the ice?"

"We keep some bottles of wine in the icehouse. And things like butter, milk, fish, and meat. If we didn't have the ice, they'd soon spoil."

As they came into the center of town George said, "Do you go to school? Is there a school here?"

Frank grinned. "A school? No. I learned to read and write before we came over, but a lot of people here can't read or write at all. The gentlemen who have enough money get private teachers or send their boys to school in England— but not their girls. The girls are just for marrying. Everybody else picks up whatever learning he can, the best way he can. Anyway, most of us always have some work to do."

"But don't you have any fun? Don't you play games or something?"

"Of course we play games! We pitch horseshoes, play marbles, tag, blindman's buff—even kissing games—just like we used to play back home."

The boys kicked at the dust in the road as they strolled through the little town. George said, "One of the sailors on the ship said that nobody here can do much of anything on Sunday. He said almost everything was against the law then. Is that true?"

Frank nodded. "It's true, all right. Folks can't work or dance, or play the fiddle, or go bowling on the green, or play checkers—we can't even go fishing or hunting on the Sabbath. Everybody has to go to church."

"Suppose you don't want to go to church?" George asked.

"Then you lie neck and heels in jail all night and work a whole week for the town. And if you stay away from

40

church twice in a row, you must pay fifty pounds of tobacco and do town work for a month."

"What happens if a man gets caught doing something he shouldn't?"

"That depends on what he did. But prob'ly he'd be put in the stocks. If he did something real bad, he might get the whipping post."

Frank squinted at the brick church some distance away. He pointed to it and said, "See that man standing in the church doorway?"

"Yes," George said. "It looks as if he has something hanging around his neck."

"He has. It's a big iron pot, and he has to stand there for two days. It's his punishment."

"For what?"

"For getting drunk."

"He must feel ashamed."

"I guess so. But not as ashamed as a man who stole a pair of breeches a week ago. He has to go to church for three Sundays with a pair of breeches tied around his neck. And he has the word 'THIEF' printed on his back."

The boys heard a man's voice calling, "George! George!" They saw a man and woman in the street. The man was beckoning.

"That's my mother and father," George said. He waved at them and began to run. "G'bye, Frank," he called. "I hope we meet again."

George rejoined his parents. His mother, a tall attractive woman with red hair, smiled at him. "You seem to have found a friend already," she said.

George nodded. "His name's Frank Thomas. He was just showing me around." He looked at his father. "Are we going to live here, Father?"

41

"Not right here, Boy. Our land is up the river. We're going to get a wagon and a couple of horses and some provisions. Then we'll be on our way."

The next day the Williams family headed north toward the country of the big plantations.

5

Cavaliers and Conflicts

Although many people came to Virginia seeking land and a new life, some were forced to come against their will. Scottish and Irish soldiers, for instance, had fought against the English king overseas. Scores of these fighters were captured in 1651 and 1653 and exiled to Virginia.

English ships also brought to Jamestown men and women who had been jailed for all sorts of offenses. Some were simply paupers, or unemployed persons. Some were thieves, pickpockets, swindlers, and other undesirables. Teen-age boys were often kidnapped in London and shipped to the colony. The kidnappers were paid by sailors or others who later traded the boys for money or land. Many people found jobs on the big Virginia plantations. A number married colonists and managed to get small plots of land where they built homes and raised food crops or tobacco. Some thieves continued to steal or to commit other crimes until they were caught and punished.

Not all newcomers came to Virginia directly from Great Britain. Men, women, and children who had first settled in the Massachusetts Bay Colony found that the laws there were too strict. They had come to America to seek freedom but found Puritan intolerance instead. Life was more miserable there than it had been in England. Scores of dissatisfied families left Massachusetts and went to live in Maryland and Virginia.

Some of these people were members of the Society of Friends, known as Quakers. In England they had wanted to worship in their own way, and they ridiculed the king's church and its ministers. They refused to pay certain taxes or to respect ranks or titles. The king did everything he could to hurt them, so hundreds of Quakers sailed away to settle in New England. They said they wanted only to worship in peace in their own way, but they interfered with the religious beliefs of other people.

The Quakers were persecuted in Massachusetts. If English ships brought Quakers to New England, the ships' captains were made to pay heavy fines. Some Quakers landed elsewhere and walked to the colony. When they began to preach, they were arrested and had their ears cut off, then they were sent away. In Boston, many were hanged.

To escape such cruelties, Quakers went to Virginia. They

soon learned they were not welcome there, either. One Virginia law provided that "Any person . . . entertaining any Quaker in or near his house, to teach or preach, shall, for every time of such entertainment, be fined five thousand pounds of tobacco."

Many Quakers were whipped in public and fined before they were ordered to leave the Virginia Colony. Gradually the Quakers began to settle in Rhode Island, because that was the only place where they were not persecuted. Years later, the Pennsylvania Colony became a Quaker haven.

Other troubles were far more serious than those involving the Quakers. In England, King Charles II declared the Virginia Colony to be a Dominion—the only such honor bestowed upon any American colony. In 1651 Parliament appointed Richard Bennett, a Virginian, to rule the colony in place of Governor William Berkeley. Berkeley resisted, but a fleet of British warships compelled him to surrender, and he went to live at his home, called Greenspring, near Jamestown.

Richard Bennett was succeeded by two other commissioners, Richard Digges and Samuel Matthews, but in 1660 Governor Berkeley was put back in power.

Sir William Berkeley was a cavalier. In earlier years he had been a good governor, but when he again took office in 1660 he was bitter, selfish, and cruel. He was loyal to the English king and didn't want the people of Virginia to have a voice in their government. In order that he could rule as he wished, he schemed to have the assembly made up of his own followers. Then, for thirteen years, he refused to permit new elections. He and his cronies ran the government. The governor was really a dictator.

Up to this time the Negroes who had been brought to the colony had worked as indentured servants. After they had served their terms—usually about five years—they were given land and were considered free people. But in 1662 there was a big demand for labor on the tobacco plantations. Not enough white men could be found to work in the houses and fields. The planters began to buy more Negroes, but they were no longer looked upon as indentured servants. They were considered to be slaves and were treated as such. This meant that they could be bought and sold, like tobacco, and that they and their children would be in bondage all their lives. They could be made to work as long and as hard as their masters desired.

In 1665 a British law prevented the colonists from buying any more white men as indentured servants. This simply increased the demand for Negro slaves, not only in Virginia, but also in all of the other American colonies.

There were severe laws regarding slaves. Sydney George Fisher, in his book, *Men, Women and Manners In Colonial Times,* wrote:

A slave was punished for being found off his plantation without a certificate from his master. He was not allowed to carry a club, a gun, or other weapon. If he resisted when corrected, it is [lawful] to kill him. If he gave false testimony, he was to have one ear nailed to the pillory, stand for an hour, and then have his ear cut off. After that the other ear was to be served in like manner, and in addition he was to receive thirty-nine lashes well laid on. Meetings and assemblies of Negroes were forbidden, and incorrigible runaways could be killed at sight.

Fisher added that most slaves in Virginia were treated

kindly, so that they "bred more rapidly and were more profitable to their masters."

The speech of the African Negroes was completely different from that of their English masters, with respect to pronunciation. The Negro said Ah for I, Vuhginia for Virginia, Yo for Your. His talk was patterned after his life and language in Africa. Many white children were raised by Negro slaves and gradually took on their speech habits. Today, some historians point out that people who speak with a Southern accent can trace it back to their colonial ancestors and their slaves.

Families with small farms did their own work and were unable to compete with the big plantations. They didn't have money to buy more land or slaves. Costs of shipping their tobacco from plantation docks were high. These small farmers began to move to the southern and western frontiers to get away from the big planters. In this way the population of the colony stretched out farther and farther.

Meanwhile, in 1651, 1660, and 1663, the English Parliament enacted new laws, known as the Navigation Acts. These laws forced the Virginia colonists to export tobacco only on English ships and only to English ports.

For years Virginia tobacco had been sold at high prices to markets in many European countries. Now it went to English merchants who paid low prices and resold it at big profits. Ships did not come often. Tobacco piled up in the Virginia warehouses and rotted before it could be shipped. What had been a rich trade became poor. Tobacco that sold for five cents a pound in 1650 was worth only half a cent by 1667. The colony was in a bad economic depression, yet the governor imposed high taxes on the people.

The colonists were both angry and helpless. They couldn't

change the English laws and they couldn't get rid of Governor Berkeley. Then came more trouble. In 1676 war parties of Susquehannock Indians swept along the Virginia frontier, killing men, women, and children, burning their homes and slaughtering their livestock.

One man whose plantation was attacked was Nathaniel Bacon, a member of the governor's council. He lived in Curles, Henrico County, and was a leading citizen of Virginia. Young Bacon met with another leader, William Byrd, to plan an attack on the Indians. Under Byrd's direction, Bacon led men into the wilderness to fight the savages.

News of this action soon reached Governor Berkeley. He had made handsome profits by fur trading with the Indians. Now this source of income was in danger. He called in a messenger.

"Get word to Nathaniel Bacon that he and his men are to return immediately," he said. "If he disobeys, he will be considered a rebel."

Bacon received the message. Instead of returning, he and his men attacked a band of hostile Indians at Occaneechee Island. They took prisoners and brought them back to the colony. The settlers hailed Bacon as a hero.

The whole colony stood solidly behind Bacon. The people demanded a new election for the House of Burgesses. Berkeley finally agreed, hoping to gain favor with the colonists. As a result of the election, many of his followers were replaced by men who were discontented with his rule. One of those newly elected was Nathaniel Bacon, whom the governor now declared to be a rebel.

When Bacon sailed down the James River to Jamestown to take his seat, Berkeley ordered cannons to be fired at his sloop to keep him from landing. That night he went ashore secretly but was captured and brought before Berkeley.

Berkeley realized that Bacon was considered a hero, and that the new House of Burgesses was unfriendly to the governor. He decided it was wise to give Bacon a parole.

"I want more than a parole!" Bacon said. "I want a commission to hunt down and destroy the Indians that have attacked our people."

"That, sir, is something I shall have to consider at length," the governor said.

Day after day the governor refused to make his decision. Suddenly Bacon mysteriously disappeared from Jamestown. Soon he returned with a small army. His men seized the ferry, the fort, and roads into and out of the village. Then they surrounded the Statehouse, where Bacon demanded his commission.

Berkeley was forced to grant his request. In addition, the new burgesses took this chance to revoke a number of objectionable laws and gave people the right to run Jamestown in their own way.

Bacon then returned to his home at Henrico and prepared to move against the Indians. Berkeley, however, organized troops to fight Bacon. After various maneuvers, the two forces clashed near Jamestown. They battled for a week, then Berkeley retreated, and Bacon and his army marched into Jamestown.

The rebels rested there for a few days. Then in a blaze of defiance, on September 19, they set fire to most of the houses and buildings. Jamestown was burned to the ground. Governor Berkeley fled across Chesapeake Bay to Accomack County.

Bacon and his men marched to Gloucester, which was being considered as a new location for the capital of the colony. In Gloucester, Bacon was stricken with malaria. He died there on October 26, 1676, and his men buried him in a secret place. It remains a secret to this day.

With Bacon gone, his revolution ended. But in many ways it was the forerunner of a greater revolution that was to take place a hundred years later, in 1776.

Governor Berkeley now wanted revenge. He ordered his soldiers to hunt down Bacon's lieutenants. Twenty-three of them were caught. Some were shot; the others, hanged. When news of these executions reached King Charles II in England the king said, "That old fool has hanged more men in that naked country than I've done for the murder of my father!"

The king sent a group of men to investigate the rebellion. After they made their report, he ordered Berkeley to return to England. Berkeley died there soon after his arrival.

In May 1680 Thomas, Lord Culpeper was sent to Virginia to rebuild Jamestown and make it into a bustling city. One historian wrote that "Culpeper swindled the people by raising and lowering the value of the coin," and that other governors also sought to grow rich at the colony's expense. However, Jamestown was reborn.

By 1697 Jamestown had a new Statehouse, a fort, a church, a powder magazine, a jail, and about thirty homes.

It was not to last. On October 31, 1698, came the cry, "Fire! Fire!" The Statehouse, the jail, and a number of other buildings were destroyed by flames. Once again much of Jamestown was left in ashes.

This time the colonists decided to move the capital. They chose a place suggested by Governor Francis Nicholson. It was called Middle Plantation and was only about seven miles from Jamestown, on the mainland.

Middle Plantation was a small, stockaded village until

after 1690. In that year Dr. James Blair, a church leader, headed a movement to start a new college. He was sent to England to get the approval of King William and Queen Mary. After many delays, in 1693 the rulers granted a charter for the founding of The College of Their Majesties, William and Mary. This is now the second oldest college in our country. The oldest is Harvard, in Cambridge, Massachusetts. By 1695 the main building, designed by Sir Christopher Wren, was completed, and students were being enrolled.

Perhaps the college was one reason the people decided to make Middle Plantation the colony's capital. Anyway, the move was made in 1699 and the name of the settlement was changed to Williamsburg in honor of King William.

It was necessary to build a new Statehouse. To get the money for it, the General Assembly made colonists pay a tax on every slave and also on every white servant who was not born in England or Wales. The building was completed in 1705. It was two stories high and shaped like the letter *H*. It was called the capitol. This was the first time the word capitol was used for a government building.

In Williamsburg and other growing towns, the church was important. The Church of England, or Episcopal Church, was the only approved church in Virginia. When Baptist preachers came to the colony, they and their followers were often attacked by angry mobs. Once someone threw a snake and a hornet's nest into a Baptist meeting. The meeting quickly ended!

The Reverend James Ireland, a Baptist minister who tried to preach in Culpeper, was jailed for disturbing the peace. Citizens tried to kill him by setting off dynamite under the floor of his cell. The explosion did only minor damage to the floor. The preacher wasn't hurt.

Then the attackers filled pods of Indian pepper with brimstone. They stuck the pods in the small space under the bottom of the jail door. Then they set the pods on fire. The smoke from the burning brimstone almost suffocated Mr. Ireland. He saved himself by putting his mouth close to cracks in the wall and sucking in the outside air.

While many Virginians took part in religious persecutions, others were concerned about equally important matters. By 1700 there were more than eighty thousand people scattered throughout the Virginia Colony. Many of these were eager to explore the unknown lands to the south. Others wanted to see what lay beyond the towering mountains that, like a high wall, hid the west.

6

Trails West

A number of colonists who left the Jamestown area made their homes near the eastern slopes of the mountains. These mountains stretched as far as one could see and looked bluer than the deep blue sky. No wonder people began to call them the Blue Ridge.

But it was not until August 1716 that Alexander Spotswood, who was then governor of the colony, decided to climb the great hills. He led a group of friends from Williamsburg to the top of the Blue Ridge.

His friends rode horseback, but Spotswood rode in a carriage as far as his country home in Germanna, near Fredericksburg. From Germanna there were no roads over which a carriage could travel, so the governor rode a horse and headed west with his companions. He was a striking figure, dressed in green velvet, wearing Russian boots, and a white plume on his wide-brimmed hat.

He and his men were followed by a number of servants and pack horses. Every now and then the explorers stopped to rest and to drink champagne, whiskey, brandy, and wine.

After many days they reached the top of the mountains. They were the first white colonists to look down upon the other side, and they were overwhelmed by the beauty of what they saw. There below, sprawling for miles, was a magnificent broad green valley. Winding through it, like a curving silver ribbon, was a wide river. Later it was learned that the Shawnee Indians, who lived in the valley, called the place Shanando, meaning "Daughter of the Skies." The white men named the valley and the river Shenandoah.

Across the valley the men could see wave after wave of mountains piled on mountains.

"They're beautiful!" one man said.

"Yes," another said. "But you can't grow tobacco on the side of a mountain. Is there no other flat land beyond this valley?"

Governor Spotswood answered. "There's plenty of good land to the west. Just now, though, it's occupied by Indians and the French."

"The French?"

"Yes. The French are spreading out. I understand they are gradually coming this way, towards the sea. We must encourage our people to cross these hills and settle in this great valley. This will provide some protection for our colonies to the east."

Spotswood led his men down the western slopes and across the river. According to one writer, before Spotswood left the mountains he carved in a rock the name of George I and named the mountain Mount George. Spotswood's friends then named the adjoining hill Mount Alexander in his honor.

Another account said that Spotswood was unable to cut the rock, so he carved his own name on a tree near the Shenandoah River. He is said to have written on a piece of paper a notice that he "took possession of this place in the name of George I, King of England."

The horses that carried Spotswood and his men up and down the rough mountains lost a number of horseshoes on the rocky ground. The men had expected this and had brought replacements. One story says that after they returned to Williamsburg, Governor Spotswood had a jeweler make a miniature golden horseshoe for each of his companions. Each shoe was decorated with jewels and bore the Latin words, *Sic Juvat Transcendere Montes,* meaning "Thus he swears to cross the mountains."

A different account says that only one miniature horseshoe like this was presented to the governor by the king, who also made Spotswood a knight.

Whichever story is correct, the fact is that Spotswood and his mountain climbers became known as the Knights of the Golden Horseshoe.

During their travels from Williamsburg to the Blue Ridge, the explorers passed many settlers' homes. They were urged to stop for food and drink and to talk about what was going on in the busy towns. Travelers were always welcome in colonial homes, for they brought news from the rest of the world.

Henry Howe, who wrote *Historical Collections of Virginia,* told about one traveler who was invited to spend the night in a stranger's log cabin. The settler's wife prepared the evening meal. It consisted of a plate of hot corn bread, several jars of home made jam, bacon, venison, pork, and chicken. There was coffee, with maple sugar for sweetening, and thick cream straight from the family cow. Foods were cooked in iron pots hanging from a movable iron bar, or crane, in the cabin's fireplace.

The house was "of the better sort of log dwelling, with two stories and two or three small windows." The traveler gave his own account of the visit.

"Soon after it grew dark," he wrote, "the hostess took down a small candle mold for three candles. It had hung from the wall on a framework just in front of the fireplace, along with a rifle, long strings of dried pumpkins, and other household articles."

When he went to bed he had to go outdoors to climb stairs to his room. "It was a fine room for astronomical observations," he said. "I could see the stars through the chinks in the logs!"

He went on, "There were two beds in the room. One was occupied by a married couple, the other by myself—but there were no curtains between. On awaking in the morning I saw two ladies cooking breakfast in my bedroom, and three gentlemen seated near the fire watching them."

Breakfast consisted of pancakes made with corn meal, bacon, and coffee. The corn meal was usually made with a grater. A grater was a homemade tin disk in which holes were punched with a nail. The disk was then nailed to a block of wood so that the side with the jagged edges of the holes was exposed. Ears of dried corn were scraped across these edges to make the corn meal.

Sometimes the meal was sifted. One kind of sifter was made of deerskin stretched tightly over a hoop, like the head of a drum. The skin was then pierced with a red-hot wire, making scores of small holes.

Most families used wooden or pewter dishes. Only the rich planters had some silver plates and bowls, or fine china that was bought in England. Wooden spoons were common, and not until the middle of the eighteenth century did forks come into general use.

Many frontier families went barefoot, even in church on Sundays. Some, though, tanned their own leather and made shoes. If no one could make real shoes, he made shoepacks. These were like moccasins, made of a single piece of leather. Often the finished shoes were blackened with a mixture of soot and lard.

Almost every colonial home had a spinning wheel. The housewife spun wool or flax and made clothes for herself and her family. On the frontier she also had to do much more than ladies living in the coastal towns. For instance, she had to learn to shoot, to hunt deer, wild turkeys, or other game. She had to slaughter hogs and cattle. She plowed and planted, helped to harvest crops, mended clothes and fences, cleaned house, cooked the meals, and did many other chores.

Most frontier homes were far apart, so neighbors didn't visit each other very often. But in a few areas where there were churches, the people came on horseback or in wagons to attend services every Sunday. They brought lunch and stayed to talk with each other about their farms, their families, and their problems.

Such visits were important, because there were few amusements for frontier families. Once, in August 1665, three actors had come to Accomack on Virginia's eastern shore. They staged a performance of "Ye Bear and Ye Cubb," perhaps the first play ever presented in the American colonies. But the players were brought into court when one Edward Martin objected to the language in the play. Mr. Martin was overruled, and he had to pay the cost of the court action.

Children played fox-in-the-warren, tag, hide and seek, and other games their parents had taught them. Most frontier children didn't have much time to play, because they had to work on the farms. There were no schools in the back country, and many boys and girls grew up without learning to read or write.

In some of the towns there were one-room schools. The local ministers were also the school teachers, and their salaries were paid in tobacco.

Two men who believed schooling was important were Benjamin Syms and Thomas Eaton, both of whom lived near Hampton. When Mr. Syms died in 1635, his will provided for money and land to establish a free school in the Virginia Colony. Thomas Eaton made a similar bequest in 1659 to build the Eaton Free School. Today, Hampton has a Syms-Eaton Museum, named in honor of these two Virginians.

Things were different on the big plantations. Some of the wealthy planters brought private tutors from England to teach their sons and daughters at home. Others sent their children to England for schooling. Sometimes indentured servants or ex-convicts were educated men and became private teachers. One boy who was taught to read and write by a former convict became a famous general and statesman. His name was George Washington.

Most houses on the big plantations were built of brick. Some had only four or five rooms, but by 1750 some were two or three stories high and had twelve rooms or more.

Most colonial homes had no running water, even in the towns. They had outdoor toilets which were often decorated and disguised as garden summerhouses.

Most colonists weren't concerned about keeping clean. A person who took more than one bath a month was unusual.

Small buildings stood near each planter's house. Some housed slaves and servants. One might be a carpenter's shop, one a blacksmith shop, another a shoemaker's. The kitchen was in a separate building. There were also stables, storehouses for supplies, an icehouse, smokehouses for preserving meat, and perhaps a shed for spinning and weaving.

The wealthy planters had slaves and servants to do the hard work. One writer said that the average planter got up quite early in the morning and drank a tankard of beer, or a julep "made of rum, water and sugar." Then he rode a horse around his plantation to inspect his crops and cattle or sheep. After that, he returned to his house and had breakfast. A typical breakfast would include cold beef or ham, cold turkey, fried hominy or cornmeal mush, and bread or toast. Hominy (from the Indian, *rockahominie*) is whole or ground kernels of dried, hulled white corn boiled in milk or water. For drinks there might be a choice of tea, coffee, chocolate, or sweet apple cider.

During the day, or in the evening, a plantation family might devote time to reading. Many wealthy men had brought or imported books from England. William Byrd, for example, had almost four thousand volumes in his home, Westover. His was considered the finest personal library in all the colonies.

The big plantations had no need for towns. They had everything they needed. They raised their own vegetables and meat. Through representatives in England, the planters bought fine furnishings which were shipped to their plantations. Some of these included beautiful rugs—but instead of putting them on the floors, the family often used them as bedspreads.

Fancy clothes were imported from England by the planters and by many families living in the towns. At Sunday church services, or at parties, the men wore ruffled lace collars and knee-length coats in red, green, purple, or some other bright color. The coats had large sleeves and were ornamented with gold sash and buttons down the front. Knee-length trousers were of different colors from the coats. The men also wore brightly colored silk stockings fastened below the knee with colored garters. They wore red, green, or blue slippers of leather or silk with gold or silver buckles. Hats were made of beaver fur and had low, round crowns and wide brims. Some had silver hatbands, and plumes were still in style.

During the early seventeen-hundreds the gentlemen also wore wigs, which were fashionable in England. For a while the wigs imitated human hair, except that they were long and had curlycues or ringlets that made them look artificial. Later they appeared in all colors and shapes. Some were even made of silk or satin and didn't look like hair at all.

The clothes of the wealthy women were even more colorful than those of the men. They still wore silk, satin, velvet, or broadcloth gowns. The most popular colors were red, scarlet, green and purple. New style dresses were parted in the middle so that the wearer's fancy, colored petticoat would show. The gowns and petticoats were huge, because they were now worn on a hoopskirt frame about six feet in dia-

61

meter. Sometimes the ladies couldn't use certain doorways or climb narrow stairs because the hoops were too big to get through.

The gentlemen and ladies spent much time enjoying themselves. Horse-racing, cock-fighting, and boxing were popular sports, and gambling was common. Fairs were held often in market places and were gay events. Sydney George Fisher wrote about one fair in Norfolk:

> Young men ran races with young women; pigs were turned loose and the whole crowd chased them among each other's legs to catch them by their greased tails. Some people were sewn up in sacks and ran races, tumbling and rolling over each other. Others raced through sugar hogsheads placed end to end with the ends out, and as the great barrels got rolling to and fro, the affair ended in nothing but "noise and confusion."
>
> Then a man would appear with a pot of hot mush, and eaters with distorted faces and tearful eyes gobbled at it to see which was the fastest. . . .

At most fairs there were fiddling contests. Fiddlers were always in demand in the towns to provide music for dancing. Dances included minuets, jigs, and reels.

One announcement in *The Virginia Gazette* in 1737 told about a forthcoming celebration on St. Andrew's Day in Hanover County. Besides horse races, "12 boys of 12 years of age would run 112 yards for a hat of the cost of 12 shillings." A pair of silver buckles would be given to the winner of a wrestling match. Prizes would be awarded to the prettiest girls. There were games and contests for people of all ages.

Sometimes men engaged in gouging, especially if they had

been drinking. In gouging, each man tried to grab locks of his opponent's hair just above his ears. If he succeeded, he would then press his thumbs into the other's eyeballs. According to the rules, he would push the eyes out of their sockets unless the victim yelled, "King's cruse!" This was the colonial equivalent of "Enough!"

Probably there were such games and dances in Williamsburg to celebrate the return of Governor Spotswood and his companions from the Shenandoah Valley. When they described the beauty and richness of the land, their news soon spread throughout the colony.

Many planters and owners of small farms were eager to get more land for tobacco and other crops. A number of former tobacco fields were useless because tobacco had robbed the earth and made it poor. But in the colony there was growing confusion about the ownership of land. The king gave thousands of acres to his favorites. Sometimes he gave one friend a part of the land he had already given to someone else. This led to all kinds of arguments about who owned what.

When word spread about the rich Shenandoah Valley, a lot of Virginia settlers thought about moving to new lands over the mountains. But it was almost ten years before many of them went. To encourage settlement, each colonist was offered four hundred acres of land in the valley. Under certain conditions, he could also get an additional thousand acres.

Hundreds of Quakers, Mennonites, Scotch-Irish, and others poured into the valley from Pennsylvania and New Jersey. By the time the Virginians pushed into the Shenandoah, homes and farms were well-established there. But all of the settlers faced new dangers.

The Indians saw their hunting grounds being turned into

farms. They began to kill the settlers and burn their homes.

In 1753 a force of French soldiers built a fort on the Allegheny River. Robert Dinwiddie, then lieutenant government of Virginia, sent a young English officer to tell the French to get out of British territory. The officer's name was George Washington.

Washington delivered the message, but the French commander told him that the French were there to stay.

The next year, 1754, young Washington and a troop of soldiers were sent to fight the French at the place where the Allegheny and Monongahela rivers joined to form the Ohio River. There the English and French fought the battle of Great Meadows. This was the beginning of the French and Indian War.

During this war, the Indians swept through the Shenandoah Valley and killed as many settlers as they could find. News of the massacres kept others from going to the valley until the French and Indians were beaten.

In 1763 a peace treaty was signed, and the war officially ended. But back in Williamsburg and other Virginia towns there was unrest. The colonists were growing angry because they felt they were being treated unfairly by the king and his government in England.

7

Politics and Patriots

As a teen-ager, George Washington had worked as a surveyor in the Virginia Colony. In 1748, when he was six-teen, he had crossed the Blue Ridge to survey some of the hundreds of thousands of acres that belonged to Lord Thomas Fairfax. These lands were later divided into fifteen large counties in Virginia and five in what is now West Virginia.

Lord Fairfax was so pleased with Washington's work that

he had him officially appointed as Surveyor of Culpeper County. The county at that time extended across the mountains into the Shenandoah Valley. Washington surveyed tracts of land for settlers moving into the valley. He also laid out Virginia towns such as Culpeper, now a thriving community seventy miles from our national capital.

In this work, George Washington met a great many people. Everyone liked him and he made a fine appearance. He was over six feet tall, with big hands and feet, light brown hair and grayish-blue eyes.

In 1756, when he was twenty-four, Washington was a candidate for election to the Virginia legislature. On election day, men, women, and children milled about in front of the Frederick County Court House. They were talking and laughing and arguing about politics. A line of men formed at the Court House, waiting to vote. Only those who owned land could do so.

Inside the building, each voter gave his name. He was then asked to speak the name of his candidate. All voting was by voice. There was no secret ballot until years later.

One after another the men called out, "George Washington . . . George Washington . . . Washington. . . ."

So George Washington was elected a member of the House of Burgesses from Frederick County. His experience as a soldier and a surveyor, his education, and his ability to get along with people would make him a good leader in the colony.

Virginia needed good leaders at this time. Bad feeling was growing between the king and the colonists. After the French and Indian War, the king decided to set up a dividing line. The colonists were to stay east of the Blue Ridge, leaving the west to the Indians. The farmers and plantation owners objected. They wanted to take up more lands in the west.

While this argument went on, a new and more serious one arose. In 1765 the king and the British Parliament imposed the first direct tax on the American colonies. This law was called the Stamp Act. It provided that tax stamps must be bought and put on such things as newspapers, playing cards, all legal documents, calendars—almost every kind of printed matter.

The colonists protested. This new law had been enacted in England where the colony had no representatives to speak in its behalf.

King George had an excuse for the Stamp Act. In effect he said, "It has cost England a great deal of money to fight the war against the French and Indians. This war was fought for the people in the colonies. Now they must help to pay for it by paying this tax."

Virginia, Massachusetts, and seven other colonies sent a protest to Parliament. It was ignored.

In the Virginia House of Burgesses in Williamsburg, one member stood up to speak. His name was Patrick Henry. He was a tall, lanky redhead, twenty-nine years old. He made a fiery speech, saying that only Virginians should be able to tax Virginians. Tax laws for Virginia should not be made by Parliament in faraway London.

Some of the other members were frightened by such revolutionary talk. They cried, "Treason! Treason!"

When their shouts died down Patrick Henry raised one arm, with a finger pointing at the ceiling. He said, "Caesar had his Brutus, Charles the First his Cromwell, and George the Third may profit by their example. If this be treason, make the most of it!"

One spectator who heard the speech was deeply impressed. He was twenty-two years old, and a student at William and Mary College. His name was Thomas Jefferson.

The colonists refused to buy English goods that were taxable under the new law. Groups called The Sons of Liberty held protest marches. In some towns they threatened to tar and feather Stamp Act officials, and the officials ran away.

When King George and Parliament heard about the strong objections, the Stamp Act was repealed in 1766. But new laws were promptly enacted to show that England had the right to tax her colonies. Parliament then put new taxes on goods imported by the colonies, such as tea.

The colonists were now more than ever united against the king. For the next few years they quarreled with his officials. In 1769 there were riots in the streets of Boston. In Williamsburg the House of Burgesses was in sympathy with the Boston rioters, so the governor closed down the assembly. Its members went to the Raleigh Tavern in Williamsburg. There George Washington led a move to stop the buying of goods and slaves from England.

All thirteen American colonies acted to show their defiance of the British tax laws. In 1773 a group of patriots disguised as Indians boarded a British ship that had just brought a load of tea to Boston. They dumped the tea into the harbor as a protest against the tea tax. This action was later called the Boston Tea Party.

The British soldiers closed the port of Boston so ships could not go in or out until the colonists paid for the lost tea. Virginia and the other colonies sent food and supplies to the people in Boston. The governors in those colonies closed the assemblies.

The Virginians suggested that all the colonies send representatives to meet in Philadelphia, Pennsylvania, to talk about their problems. This meeting was held September 5, 1774. All colonies except Georgia took part. This was the first session of what became known as the Continental Congress.

Among the leaders from Virginia were Thomas Jefferson, Patrick Henry, and George Mason.

There was more and more talk about resistance and rebellion. The talk turned to action on April 18, 1775. A band of armed citizens battled a troop of British soldiers at Lexington, Massachusetts. This was the beginning of an all-out war between Great Britain and the American colonies.

Virginia adopted a motto *Sic Semper Tyrannis* (Thus Always To Tyrants). Patrick Henry, commanding the Virginia militia, sent out a call to arms. Among the quickest to respond were the first "Minute Men" raised in Virginia. From Orange, Fauquier, and Culpeper counties, 350 of these swashbucklers met in the town of Culpeper. Their flag became famous. At its top was the design of a ribbon with the words, "The Culpeper Minute Men." In the center was the figure of a coiled rattlesnake with twelve rattles and the words, "Liberty Or Death!" Below the snake was the warning, "Don't Tread On Me." The head of the snake symbolized Virginia. The twelve rattles represented the other twelve colonies.

The Culpeper Minute Men wore green hunting shirts with the words "Liberty Or Death!" in large white letters across the chests. They had bucktails in their hats, tomahawks and knives in their belts. Years later, United States Senator John Randolph, a noted Virginian, said that these fighters were "raised in a minute, armed in a minute, marched in a minute, fought in a minute, and vanquished in a minute." They marched to Williamsburg to join other volunteers.

On June 7, 1776, at a meeting of the Second Continental Congress, Richard Henry Lee of Virginia moved a resolution "that these united colonies are, and of right ought to be, free and independent states." John Adams of Massachusetts seconded the motion.

Acting upon this resolution, the Congress on July 4 approved adoption of a Declaration of Independence. The Declaration gave the reasons for fighting the king. It also declared that the colonies were no longer under English rule. Several people helped to prepare the Declaration. They were Benjamin Franklin representing Pennsylvania, John Adams and Roger Sherman of Massachusetts, Robert R. Livingston of New York, and Thomas Jefferson of Virginia. Most of the wording was composed by Jefferson, and it included the term "United States of America" for the first time.

The Declaration was signed by fifty-six men. Seven were from Virginia. They were Richard Henry Lee, Francis Lightfoot Lee, Thomas Jefferson, Benjamin Harrison, George Wythe, Thomas Nelson, Jr., and Carter Braxton.

Hundreds of patriots rushed to join the American forces under command of General George Washington.

At first the fighting centered in New England and the Middle Atlantic states. Gradually it spread southward. The Americans won some battles. The British won others. In 1780 Thomas Jefferson, then governor of Virginia, made Richmond the capital of the new state. On January 5, 1781, a British force commanded by Benedict Arnold captured Richmond. He burned several of its buildings, then marched to Portsmouth.

In May the British again planned to take Richmond. Governor Jefferson adjourned the assembly. He ordered its members to meet in Charlottesville on May 24. He went to Charlottesville with a number of famous Revolutionary leaders, including Patrick Henry, Benjamin Harrison, Richard Henry Lee, and Thomas Nelson. They stayed at Monticello, Jefferson's beautiful home, near the town. There they believed they were safe—but they were really in danger. Other members of the legislature stayed in Charlottesville.

General Cornwallis, commander of the British troops, was

then in southern Virginia. He gave top secret orders to Colonel Banastre "Bloody" Tarleton to lead 250 soldiers to Charlottesville. There they were to seize Jefferson and the members of the Virginia Assembly, with their supplies, plans, and valuable papers.

Tarleton and his men marched to Louisa County without being detected by the Americans. On the night of June 3 they stopped at the Cuckoo Tavern, only forty miles from Charlottesville. Tarleton was now sure that he could take Jefferson by complete surprise. If he succeeded, the American cause would suffer a great blow.

While Tarleton and his men were at the Cuckoo Tavern, they were watched by a young Virginia soldier, Captain Jack Jouett. Jouett was a native of Charlottesville. He was six feet four inches tall and weighed about two hundred twenty pounds—a young giant.

Of course he didn't know what Tarleton's orders were. He guessed, however, that the British were on their way to Charlottesville. He knew he must warn Jefferson—but he also knew that if he followed the roads he might arrive too late. He would have to make a night ride through rough country.

Young Jouett leaped upon his horse about ten o'clock and galloped into the darkness. There were no signs to guide him, no lanterns to light the way. Horse and rider sped up and down hills, across flat land. They forded streams and slashed through ravines and thick underbrush. Bushes whipped the man's legs and the horse's flanks. Thorns tore through Jouett's pants and skin, sending trickles of blood down to his ankles. Low branches scraped his face. Some of the cuts were to leave ugly permanent scars.

Soon after Jouett left the scene, Tarleton and his soldiers began their night march to Charlottesville. They made two short stops to rest. At one point they came upon a few Americans with twelve supply wagons. The British seized and burned the wagons, then continued on their way to capture Jefferson and the Virginia lawmakers.

When the first light of dawn appeared on June 4, Jack Jouett was riding up the long hill to Monticello. He had galloped forty miles through wild country. His clothes were torn, his face bleeding, his hair tousled. His eyes were red from the wind and from lack of sleep. His sweating horse was covered with lather.

Jouett banged on the door of Jefferson's home. A surprised Negro servant answered the knocks. In a few moments Jefferson himself appeared. The weary soldier blurted out his warning about the British. Quickly Jefferson summoned his friends. Then Jack Jouett rode into Charlottesville and roused the other members of the legislature. Within a short time they fled from Charlottesville.

Jouett had beaten the British by at least three hours. By the time "Bloody" Tarleton arrived to spring his trap, there was no one for him to catch.

Jack Jouett's ride was longer, harder, and more important than that of Paul Revere in Massachusetts. Yet Jouett's ride is little known, and Revere's became famous. If it had not been for Jouett, the British would have captured some of the most important leaders of the American Revolution, and the outcome of the war might have been different.

8

End and Beginning

Not all of the important battles of the Revolution were fought in the east. West of the Blue Ridge there were countless miles of land. Some was occupied by British forces, and they encouraged the Indians to kill American settlers on the western frontier.

Part of this Virginia frontier was called by the Indian name, Kentucky, meaning "the dark and bloody ground." Kentucky settlers built stockaded forts to protect themselves from the British and Indians, but they were steadily overrun and either killed or driven from their homes.

One of these settlers was George Rogers Clark, a twenty-six-year-old redhead, who decided to organize a force to fight back. Clark was born near what is now Charlottesville, Virginia. He went to Williamsburg, and with the help of Governor Patrick Henry he assembled about two hundred Virginians to march west into the Northwest Territory, known as the Illinois country.

Clark knew that the British and their Indian allies used some of the towns in the Illinois country as hiding places from which they launched raids on the settlers. He led his men to the Ohio and Cumberland rivers, then marched overland to the target towns. In night attacks he caught the British and Indians completely by surprise and captured Kaskaskia, Cahokia, and Vincennes with little difficulty.

The British recaptured Vincennes but were again defeated by Clark, who sent the British commander back to Williamsburg as a prisoner of war. Gradually the settlers began to move back into Kentucky and other western lands.

Clark's capture of the vast Northwest Territory was one of the boldest exploits in American history. Virginia proceeded to annex this territory as the county of Illinois. Other colonies objected and wanted to claim part of the land, but Virginia insisted that the territory was "won by a Virginia army, commanded by a Virginia officer, put in the field at Virginia's expense."

However, in 1782, to avoid further conflicts among the colonies, the Virginia legislature ceded the entire area to the nation.

In 1783 a peace treaty signed by the Americans and the English provided that each country should keep whatever land it held at the end of the war. If George Rogers Clark had not conquered the Northwest Territory, the western boundary of the United States would have been fixed at the Allegheny Mountains. Because of his bold acts, the boundary was set at the Mississippi River, giving our country what are now the states of Illinois, Indiana, Michigan, Ohio, and Wisconsin.

The Virginia legislature gave Clark 8,000 acres of land and each of his soldiers 108 acres, for a total of 150,000 acres in what is now the state of Indiana.

Although the formal peace treaty was signed in 1783, the war actually ended October 19, 1781, when General Cornwallis surrendered the British army to General Washington at Yorktown, Virginia.

The colonies had won their freedom from England. They were now states—but not yet *united* states. Each considered itself a separate unit. Each was jealous of the others. There were quarrels about states' rights and privileges. Continental paper money became almost worthless. It took a bushel of money to buy a bushel of corn. Soldiers who came home from the war had no jobs. They had no money to pay their debts, and many were thrown into debtors' prisons. In Massachusetts, mobs of angry veterans broke open the jails and closed down the courts. People were losing faith in the Articles of Confederation.

The Articles of Confederation had been written after the war with England began. They were adopted by the states in 1781. They were a kind of agreement that was intended to help the thirteen colonies govern themselves. The Articles granted certain powers to the Continental Congress, but this meant little because the Congress wasn't permitted to tax the citizens or do other things to raise needed money.

In the face of the postwar troubles, the Continental Con-

gress called a meeting in Philadelphia to make the Articles of Confederation stronger.

The meeting was held in Independence Hall, where the Declaration of Independence had been signed. The leader of the meeting was General George Washington. It was decided that instead of patching up the Articles of Confederation, they should write a new document.

The big question was: "Will we set up a strong Federal government that will be controlled by the people, or will we have a collection of independent states?"

After days of arguments and discussions, it was decided to draw up a Constitution of the United States. To a great extent it was based upon a proposal called the Virginia Plan, written by James Madison of King George County, Virginia. Madison, who later became President of the United States, has been called the Father of the Constitution.

After the Constitution was drafted, it had to be sent to the states for ratification, or approval. In June 1788 a state convention met in Richmond to decide whether Virginia would approve the Constitution or not.

James Madison was a leader in fighting for approval. Patrick Henry and some others were against it. At the Shockoo Courthouse in Richmond, Patrick Henry shouted his objections. Outside, lightning flashed and thunder crashed. Henry wore a red wig that rested loosely on top of his head. Every few minutes he would reach up and spin the wig around!

Finally, Madison agreed to offer certain amendments, and Virginia ratified the Constitution by a vote of 89 to 79. She was tenth in the order of states that approved.

Officially, the Constitution took effect on March 4, 1789.

On April 30, 1789, George Washington was elected the first President of the United States.

Virginia became the mother of Presidents. After Washington, the Virginians who have held the presidency are Thomas Jefferson, James Madison, James Monroe, William Henry Harrison, John Tyler, Zachary Taylor, and Woodrow Wilson.

Today Virginia offers something to everybody. For recreation it has beautiful beaches, parks, rivers, and mountains. Boating, fishing, hunting, golf, and horse-racing are popular sports.

Cattle and hogs, along with tobacco, corn, and peanuts, bring in millions of dollars each year. Virginia is blessed with abundant forests and is the home of some of the nation's finest furniture makers. Coal and other minerals are part of the state's rich natural resources.

Virginia is proud of her many colleges, universities, and other educational institutions.

Manufacturing provides employment for more people than any other industry. The state's chief products include chemicals, textiles, lumber, furniture, foods, ships, tobacco, and clothing.

Jamestown, Williamsburg, and Richmond, the state's three successive capitals, are symbols of Virginia's great cultural heritage. The Virginia Museum of Fine Arts in Richmond has chapters and cultural programs in all parts of the state. Outdoor pageants and plays are famous. Virginia has art schools, music schools, symphony orchestras, and theaters offering a variety of programs.

After Patrick Henry died in 1799, a sealed envelope was found among his papers. Inside was a resolution condemning the Stamp Act of 1765—but on the back of the resolution, Mr. Henry wrote this about America's independence:

Whether this will prove a blessing or a curse will depend upon the use our people make of the blessings which a gracious God has bestowed on us. If they are wise, they will be great and happy. If they are of a contrary character, they will be miserable. Righteousness alone can exalt a nation. Reader, whoever thou art, remember this; and in thy sphere, practice virtue thyself and encourage it in others.

These words can well apply to our own day and age. Thanks to Patrick Henry, George Washington, Thomas Jefferson, and other far-seeing men, Virginia may justly be proud of her glorious history—a history that sets her apart forever as the place where our great nation began.

Index

ABOUT THE AUTHOR AND THE ARTIST

HARRY EDWARD NEAL was born in Pittsfield, Massachusetts. He spent thirty-one years in the United States Secret Service and retired as Assistant Chief in 1957 to devote his full time to writing. He has written numerous short stories and articles for national magazines and is also the author of more than twenty nonfiction books, mostly for young people. He has lectured and taught classes at writers' conferences.

Mr. Neal and his wife, Berniece, who is also an author, lecturer, and teacher, live in Culpeper, Virginia.

JULES GOTLIEB is a native New Yorker. He studied art at the National Academy of Fine Arts, the Pennsylvania Academy, and the Art Students League of New York. He acquired his first art studio at the age of sixteen.

Mr. Gotlieb was an art director for a lithography firm but gave this up to concentrate on illustrating for *Cosmopolitan, Redbook,* and other national magazines. He now devotes most of his time to illustrating books and jackets.